God, How Can I Know You?

Written by: Fayth Silveus

ISBN: 9781090650801

I would like to dedicate this book to God. Without God in my life I do not know where I would be today. God has walked with me through many difficult times and through those difficult times I have grown to know Him in a deeper way. I have learned to rely on Him and to seek Him to help me with each step and each breath. I have learned to allow Him to carry me when I cannot walk myself.

Looking in the Bible, God's Holy Word, has allowed me to hear Him speak.

God, thank you for being love and for loving me so much that you would send your Son to die for me! That is the true definition of love, that You would send Your Son to die for me. I could never do anything to deserve this amazing gift, however I do accept it with open arms!

I would also like to dedicate the book my husband Chad, my son Nilsson, and my daughter Violet. God has blessed me with the best family ever!

Chad, thank you for always striving to do what is right in God's eyes. You are an amazing example of a Godly man and I am blessed to have you as my husband. I love you with all of my heart!

Nilsson and Violet, thank you for being the best children that a mom could ask for. I love you more than you will ever know!

I would like to thank Coach Bryon Weinstein for taking me to Word of Life Island Basketball Camp where I met God for the very first time and gave my life to Him, and for being an excellent example of a Godly man to many generations of students and athletes.

I would like to thank Pastor Shane Davis for showing me the true nature of God's character. For showing me that God is love and for showing me the depth of God's love for me by continually challenging me to look in the Bible for all the answers to the questions that I had.

I pray that the words in this book will help parents teach their children who God is. I pray that children will learn the loving nature of our Almighty God!

Parents,

It is often difficult for children to understand who God is. They understand who their mommy and daddy are because they can see them and touch them and hear their voice. They can interact with them in a way that is familiar and comfortable. When it comes to understanding who God is, children cannot rely on the senses of sight, hearing, or touch. They must rely on the truth that is written in the Bible to guide them and teach them who God is.

Many children struggle with understanding who God is. As parents, we often feel ill equipped to answer all of the questions about who God is and how we can be so certain. In those moments, when your child is asking you questions that you cannot answer, remember that there is a book with all of the answers that you will ever need. The goal of this book is to point you to the one book that has all of the answers that we need, the Bible.

Fayth Silveus

Table of Contents

I know my mommy.
She holds my hand,
And always helps,
Me understand.

I know my daddy.
He hugs me tight,
And makes me feel,
It's all alright.

But God, how do I get to know
You?
How can I know that You are
true?
I can't see Your face or feel
Your touch.
How can I know You and love
You so much?

I hear my mommy call the
Bible Your Holy Word.
I put my ear up to it, but
guess what I heard?
Nothing, nada, not a sound!
I'll try it again when there's
no one around.

It's a really big book.
The words are so small.
You must have a lot to say.
My mommy and daddy,
Say that I,
Should read it every day.

Where can I start?
What can I do?
Father God,
How can I know You?

I like to draw,
And make things like art.
My mom says I'm really good.
She says I got,
This gift from You.
Then she says I should.
Open the Bible to Genesis.
You are an artist too.
I read about creation.
I saw what You can do.
Wow! I'm impressed by You!

You simply spoke and light appeared.
This makes me really glad.
You see, I get scared in the dark,
And then I get so sad.
But daddy turns the nightlight on.
To show me it's okay.
I guess my daddy's just like you.
Protecting me today.

You made the land and waters
too.
The plants and trees were
made by You.

How did You think of the
animals to make?
There are just so many!
Were You so exhausted?
Is it true they all were
friendly?
Did the dog and cat play nice
together?
If we did not sin would that
last forever?

Were You really sad when the
ones you gave life,
The man named Adam and Eve
his wife,
Ate the fruit from the tree,
Then hid from You,
So You could not see,
That their sin was true?

My mommy gets sad when I do
not obey,
When I choose not to listen
and go my own way.
She punishes me, I sit in time
out.
It gives me time to think
about,
How I can listen and obey her
voice.
And next time make a better
choice.

When You closed Eden, You did the same too.
For Adam and Eve didn't listen to You.
But You didn't leave them and walk away.
Instead You went with them and blessed them each day.
You're just like my mommy and daddy today!
God, I don't know what to say,
Except, I really am getting to know You today!
I see Your heart is full of love for everyone You've made.
And even if we disobey Your love will never fade!

My daddy said You made a
plan,
To overcome sin and unite us
again.
He says it was a sacrifice,
That did not make You feel so
nice.
But Your love for me was very
strong,
So, You stuck to your plan
and went along!

You sent your son Jesus into
this world,
To live a sinless life,
He was fully God and fully
man,
And He faced great strife.
He was faced with sin, yet He
turned away.
He never made a mistake.
You sacrificed Your Son for
me.
That's a love You cannot fake!

You sent Your son to die for
me,
To cover my sin and set me
free.
To make a way back to You.
Because You love me so.
To show me that Your love is
true.
To help me learn to know,
Who You are, who You really
are,
My Father with love to give.
An artist and creator,
Who died so I can live!

Back to the question I asked
before,
Father God, how can I know
You more?

I think I have an idea now,
Of how to know You more.
When I open my Bible,
Your Holy Word,
I'm opening up a door.
A door to see who You are,
And what I mean to You.
A window to watch from afar,
A Father whose love is true.

If you do not know where to begin.
Here are some places to look.
Just remember God's Holy Word,
Fills the entire Book!

1 John 4:8 – Whoever does not love does not know God, because God is love.

1 John 4:16 – And so we know and rely on the love God has for us. God is love. Whoever lives in love lives in God, and God in them.
Psalm 36:7 – How priceless is your unfailing love, O God! People take refuge in the shadow of your wings.

Psalm 86:5 – You, Lord, are forgiving and good, abounding in love to all who call to you.

Psalm 136:26 – Give thanks to the God of heaven. His love endures forever.

John 3:16 – For God so loved the word that he gave his one and only Son, that whoever believes in him shall not perish but have eternal life.
Romans 5:8 – But God demonstrates His own love for us in this: While we were still sinners, Christ died for us.

Made in the USA
Middletown, DE
18 November 2021